Calling T
Are Not .
They were

Change your life by changing your circumstances

Barb Witt

Onwards and Upwards Publications, Berkeley House,
11 Nightingale Crescent, West Horsley, Surrey KT24 6PD

www.onwardsandupwards.org

ISBN: 978-1-907509-36-0
Cover design: Leah-Maarit

Printed in the UK

About the Author

Barb Witt is from the southern state of Arkansas, U.S.A., where she enjoyed a record-breaking career in basketball. Still holding scoring records at her high school, she was selected to the All-State and Arkansas High School All Star teams.

She is tied for the all-time state record of most points in a single game. She also holds the state record for most points averaged/game in a season (six-on-six).

Barb continued to play in university on a team ranked 8th nationally in the American Athletic Union.

Her Bachelor of Science degree is in Biology/Physical Education with further training in Medical Technology. She is a registered Biomedical Scientist in the UK.

Barb was ordained in 1998 through Faith Ministries International, and as an associate, has spoken in meetings and churches in the UK and Bermuda.

Through her own ministry, she teaches the principles of faith, abundance and victorious Christian living in the Word of God, via meetings, conferences, churches, seminars, Bible schools, prisons and the VICTORIES IN FAITH publication.

Dedication

This book is lovingly dedicated to my mother, Rachel Witt. Her love, encouragement and strength have been a guiding influence in my life. Her life continues to be a rich blessing to all who know her.

When I was in high school, she would drive me to the gymnasium to prepare for a basketball game that evening. Being a high school basketball star in her own right, she would always remind me of these words before getting out of the car:

> *If you think you are beaten, you are;*
> *If you think you dare not, you don't*
> *If you'd like to win, but think you can't,*
> *It's almost a cinch that you won't.*
> *If you think you'll lose, you're lost*
> *For out in the world we find*
> *Success begins with a fellow's will;*
> *It's all in the state of mind!*
> *Life's battles don't always go*
> *To the strongest or fastest man;*
> *But sooner or later the man who wins*
> *Is the man who thinks he can!*

- Walter D. Wintle

These words are in agreement with the Word of God:

Proverbs 23:7
For as he thinketh in his heart, so is he...

The integrity and life of giving that both of my parents lived out before me have established principles of success and blessing in my life long before I was aware they were in God's Word.

Proverbs 1:8-9

My son, hear the instruction of thy father, and forsake not the law of thy mother: For they shall be an ornament of grace unto thy head, and chains about thy neck.

Calling Those Things

Contents

Calling Those Things

Foreword

Many Christians live their entire lives subject to negative circumstances, and some even believe it is the will of God for them.

We do not have to live subject to the curse and all of the effects of sin that Satan brought upon the earth. Sickness, lack and defeat on any level are included in this curse (Deuteronomy 28). This is not the will of God for us because Jesus has redeemed us from it (Galatians 3:13-14). We are to rule and reign in life by Jesus Christ (Romans 5:17).

God has never accepted negative circumstances as permanent, and He has shown us throughout His Word how to change them. Someone might say, "Yes, but that was God." God has not left us here powerless at the mercy of the devil. He created man in His likeness and image and gave him dominion over the earth and everything in it (Genesis 1:26-28). God intended for man to take dominion over his circumstances and not be subject to them. How? By releasing his faith with words, speaking what he desired instead of accepting as permanent what he was faced with.

God created the universe and everything in it with words. That is why it will respond to words - *your* words. Faith does not 'wait until it can see it' to say it.

In order to change what you have, you must speak what you desire, based on the promises of God.

Bible faith calls things that are not (seen) as though they (already) were in existence. Understanding this principle and how to apply it to your circumstances is fundamental to manifesting the promises of God in your life.

It is my desire that this book will inspire and equip you to begin changing some things around you in order that you will enjoy the good life Jesus came to give us.

Introduction

Romans 4:17, emphasis added

...(as it is written, 'I have made thee a father of many nations') before him whom he believed, even God, who quickeneth the dead, <u>and calleth those things which be not as though they were</u>.

This is one of the most misunderstood concepts of faith in the Bible. It is not a modern, man-made doctrine created by 'faith preachers' like myself. Paul admitted he was a faith preacher when he wrote:

Romans 10:8, emphasis added

But what saith it? 'The word is nigh thee, even in thy mouth, and in thy heart' (that is, <u>the word of faith which we preach</u>).

Notice in the middle of Romans 4:17 Paul says, "even God, who quickeneth the dead..." The old English word 'quickeneth' means 'makes alive'.

How does He do that?

It is further expanded in the Amplified Bible where Paul goes on to explain:

...(God) who gives life to the dead and speaks of the nonexistent things that [He has foretold and promised] as if they [already] existed.

God speaks of the nonexistent things (in the physical realm) as if they already existed (in the physical realm).

Are there some things in your life that have died and need to be made alive again?

The principle of *calling those things which be not as though they were* is not something man has chosen, it is something God has chosen.

I Corinthians 1:27-28, emphasis added

But God hath chosen the foolish things of the world to confound the wise; and God hath chosen the weak things of the world to confound the things which are mighty; and base things of the world, <u>and things which are despised, hath God chosen, yea, and things which are not, to bring to nought things that are...</u>

We find a similar statement in Hebrews 11:3:

...so that things which are seen were not made of things which do appear.

In other words, things which are seen with the physical eye are made of things which you cannot see with the physical eye. The spiritual realm gives birth to things in the physical realm.

God speaks of the nonexistent things (in the physical realm) as if they already existed (in the physical realm).

This is God's standard operational procedure. This is the lifestyle of God and the way He operates by faith throughout the Bible.

Who are we to question it?

We are to order our lifestyle in the same manner if we are going to be biblical.

Bible scholars tell us that the earlier in the Bible you find a principle used, the more significance it has. You do not have to go very far in the Bible before you find this principle in operation. God Himself instituted this principle in the first chapter of Genesis when He created the heavens and the earth.

God said what He wanted, not what He already had.

Eleven times in the very first chapter of Genesis, God enforces this principle of *calling those things which be not as though they were.*

Genesis 1:1-3

In the beginning God created the heaven and the earth. And the earth was without form, and void; and darkness was upon the face of the deep. And the spirit of God moved upon the face of the waters. And God said, Let there be light: and there was light.

The original Hebrew literally says, "Light be, and light was."

Notice, when there was nothing visible but darkness, God said, "Let there be light." He did not wait until there was light

13

before He said, "Let there be light." That would be like waiting for some heat from the fireplace before you put in some wood.

God did not declare what already existed - darkness. He did not look at the darkness and just wish it were light and contemplate how He was going to get some light. He did not say, "It is really dark out here; it would be nice to have some light, but I can't say it is light while it is still dark." If God had continued to say, "It is dark", that is what He would have continued to have, no matter how much He had wanted to change the situation. He did not "call it like it is".

I am about to make a very important statement and one you should not ever forget if you want to live a victorious Christian life: *God said what he wanted, not what he already had.*

Hebrews 11:3

Through faith we understand that the worlds were framed by the word of God...

How did God frame the worlds?

Through faith, by speaking His creative Word - *calling those things which be not as though they were.*

Job 22:28

Thou shalt also decree a thing, and it shall be established unto thee: and the light shall shine upon thy ways.

'To decree' means 'to fix or appoint', 'to set or constitute by edict or in purpose'. It does not say, "It shall be established unto thee, and then you shall decree it." No! You decree a thing first and *then* it shall be established unto you. You *call those things which be not as though they were.*

Our Father of Faith: Abraham

Further on in the book of Genesis we see God use this principle again to produce the promised son, Isaac, to Abram and Sarai. It is actually this event in Abram's life that Paul is referring to in our text scripture, Romans 4:16-17.

As you know, Abram and Sarai were well beyond the child-bearing age and, to make matters worse, Sarai had been barren all of her life. If God had not used the principle of *calling those things which be not as though they were*, Isaac would never have been born, regardless of God's will and their desire to have a child.

Genesis 13:16

And I will make thy seed as the dust of the earth: so that if a man can number the dust of the earth, then shall thy seed also be numbered.

At this point Abram does not have a revelation of what God is in the process of doing. Instead of getting into agreement with what God has spoken, he continues to 'call things that are as though they are'. He just tells it like it is. For example:

Genesis 15:2, emphasis added

And Abram said, Lord God, what wilt thou give me, <u>seeing I go childless</u>, and the steward of my house is this Eliezer of Damascus?"

15

Most Christians today would ask, "What's wrong with that? He's just being real. He would be lying if he said anything else. He was just telling is like it is."

Yes, he was telling it like it was and that was a major reason nothing was changing for him in this area. When people say they are just "being real", they really mean that they believe what they see, hear and feel more than they believe the Word of God. 'Being real' will keep you defeated at best or get you killed at worst. You need to 'get real' on God's Word if you are going to live victoriously in this life. God has given us His Word to benefit us.

> He is giving us an object lesson on how we must operate in order to change the circumstances we currently have, into the circumstances we desire.

In Genesis 17, God speaks to Abram again when he is 99 years old. God continues to *call those things which be not as though they were.*

Genesis 17:4-5

As for me, behold, my covenant is with thee, and thou shalt be a father of many nations. Neither shall thy name any more be called Abram, but thy name shall be Abraham; for a father of many nations have I made thee.

Notice this last statement to Abram: "For a father of many nations *have I made thee.*" That is in the past tense. As far as God was concerned it was already done.

Wait just a minute here! Have we caught God telling a lie?

He was telling a man who is ninety-nine years old and whose wife is ninety years old that he was (already) a father of many nations. God had to explain that it was with Isaac, born of Sarah, that He would establish His covenant, not Ishmael.

Why didn't God just wait until Isaac was born and then call Abraham a father after the fact? That is what most people would have done. They would say, "I can't say I'm a father of many nations when I'm not yet. That would be telling a lie."

God is clearly trying to tell us that "telling it like it is" is not the way He operates. He is giving us an object lesson on how we must operate in order to change the circumstances we currently have into the circumstances we desire.

When God said to Abraham, a "father of many nations have I made thee", in the mind of God it was already done. Now He was endeavouring to get Abraham into agreement with Him. One of the things He did was to change His name from Abram which means 'exalted father' to Abraham - 'father of a multitude'. He also changed Sarai's name to 'Sarah', meaning 'princess', to include her in the promise.

From now on, every time Abraham hears his name called, he hears, "father of a multitude". His thoughts begin to come into agreement with God. New thoughts are being established in his mind: "I am (present tense) the father of a multitude."

I can just hear his so-called friends now. "There goes crazy Abraham, ninety-nine years old with a barren wife who is ninety, calling himself the father of a multitude." Who do you think bore the brunt of every joke in the community?...

17

> You are fully persuaded when what you see and
> hear does not affect what you believe in God's
> word.

It took a little while for Abraham to become fully persuaded and get in agreement with God, but once he did, Isaac was born within one year.

What does it mean to be 'fully persuaded'?

You are fully persuaded when what you see and hear does not affect what you believe in God's Word.

Genesis 21:5

And Abraham was an hundred years old, when his son Isaac was born unto him.

The Message Translation of this account says:

Romans 4:17

Abraham was first named "father" and then "became" a father.

No, we have not caught God in a lie. He is teaching us how He operates by faith and how we must operate in order to lay hold of His promises - *calling those things which be not as though they were.*

What is a Lie?

Some would accuse God of "denying reality" when He refused to accept the darkness in the earth and called for light in Genesis 1. Was God lying when He said, "light be" while there was darkness all around Him? "Light be" was contrary to everything around Him; did that mean it was a lie?

Let's put this in a context that is closer to home. Is someone lying when they say, "I'm healed" when it appears to us they are not?

According to the dictionary 'a lie' is 'a falsehood uttered for the purpose of deception'. If one attempts to deceive someone into believing something that is not true, by definition it is a lie.

Just because you don't presently have it, or see it physically, does not mean it does not exist.

God's Word is the highest form of truth. When you speak and believe in agreement with His Word it cannot be a lie, whether you can see any evidence of it in the natural yet or not. Abraham had to ignore what he could see in his physical circumstances and believe what God had promised. He struggled with this for twenty-four years and God had to repeat His promise to him over and again. It may have been a 'fact' that he and his wife were beyond childbearing age physically and could not have children, but it was not the truth. God's Word to him was the truth.

Genesis 17:19

And God said, 'Sarah thy wife shall bear thee a son indeed; and thou shalt call his name Isaac: and I will establish my covenant with him for an everlasting covenant and with his seed after him.'

It took a while for God to get Abraham to the place where he could believe God's Word instead of what he could see around him.

> The eye of faith looks at what the Word says, not what circumstances are telling you.

Just because you don't presently have it or see it physically does not mean it does not exist. It just exists in the spiritual realm that you cannot see with your physical eyes. That's why we have to develop "the eye of faith". The eye of faith looks at what the Word of God says, not what circumstances are telling you.

Joseph

In Genesis 39, we see another example of God *calling those things which be not as though they (already) were.*

Genesis 39:1-2, emphasis added

And Joseph was brought down to Egypt; and Potiphar, an officer of Pharaoh, captain of the guard, an Egyptian, bought him of the hands of the Ishmaelites, which had brought him down thither. And the LORD was with Joseph, <u>and he was a prosperous man</u>...

Wait just a minute... Have we caught God in another lie?

Joseph had been brought to Egypt and was standing in a slave market... with nothing. Yet God called him 'a prosperous man'. God was not 'calling things that were as though they were'. He was not 'telling it like it is'. He was looking through the eye of faith.

God did not wait until Joseph was promoted second to Pharaoh, wearing fine clothes and jewellery, overseeing all the money and all the food in the nation, to then declare, "Joseph, now you are a prosperous man." No. God called him prosperous before there was any evidence of it in his life, and because He did, *it was*. The manifestation of it eventually appeared.

Isaiah 46: 9-10, emphasis added

Remember the former things of old: for I am God, and there is none else; I am God, and there is none like me, <u>declaring the end from the beginning</u>...

Establishing the Basics of Faith

A basic but very important principle of living by faith that you must understand from the outset is this: *When you are operating in faith, you are not dealing with the unknown. You are dealing with the unseen.*

Just because something is unseen to us in the physical realm does not mean it does not exist. The spiritual realm is actually more real than the physical realm. The spiritual unseen realm gave birth to the physical realm; therefore the spiritual realm supersedes the physical realm (Genesis 1). It may not exist yet in the physical realm but it already exists in the spirit realm.

When you are operating by faith, you are not dealing with the unknown; you are dealing with the unseen.

I'm going to make another statement that you need to keep at the forefront of your mind: *Circumstances do not change God's Word. God's Word changes circumstances.*

Jesus said:

John 6:63

...the words that I speak unto you, they are spirit, and they are life.

Most Christians have not been taught to believe God's Word over and above what they can see, feel and hear. Most of them think like this: "When I see it, I will believe it" or "When I see it first then I will say I have it." That is why they still don't see it or have it. They will never believe anything that has not already happened. Remember 'Doubting Thomas' who would not believe the other disciples' eye witness account that Jesus had been raised from the dead until he physically saw and touched him. Jesus called him faithless.

Circumstances do not change God's Word. God's Word changes circumstances.

John 11:40, emphasis added
Said I not unto thee, that, if thou wouldest <u>believe</u>, thou shouldest <u>see</u> the glory of God.

Jesus said that first you must believe before you see. In John 20, (Doubting) Thomas refused to believe Jesus had been raised from the dead until he saw Him and touched Him. He refused to believe what he had not seen. Jesus rebuked him for being faithless and said to him:

> *Thomas, because thou has seen me, thou hast believed; blessed are they that have not seen, and yet have believed.*

If you want to be blessed, you have to believe the Word of God before you can see the promise manifested in your life. Faith says, "I believe it; therefore I have it (now)."

Hebrews 11:1, emphasis added
<u>Now</u> faith is the substance of things hoped for, <u>the evidence of things not seen</u>.

23

The Amplifed Bible puts it this way:

Hebrews 11:1, Amplified, emphasis added

Now faith is the assurance (the confirmation, <u>the title deed</u>) of the things [we] hope for, being <u>the proof of things</u> [we] <u>do not see</u> and <u>the conviction of their reality</u> [faith perceiving as real fact what is not revealed to the senses].

Do you confess that heaven is your future destiny now, even though you have never seen it? Or are you going to wait until you can see heaven to declare, "I believe it now that I see it"?

No! You do not have to see heaven to believe it is your inheritance. Why? Your faith is developed in that area. You believe the evidence of the Word of God alone without having to see it first. Now you need to develop your faith in other areas of God's Word and what already belongs to you.

If you can already see it and you already have it, faith is not required. Faith is the evidence it exists in the unseen realm.

II Corinthians 4:17-18

For our light affliction, which is but for a moment, worketh for us a far more exceeding and eternal weight of glory; <u>while we look not at the things which are seen, but at the things which are not seen</u>; for the things which are seen are temporal; but the things which are not seen are eternal.

If you can already see it and you already have it, faith is not required.

Paul is telling us that things which are seen and need to be changed are temporary. This means that the things which are not seen (with the physical eye) are not temporary; they are eternal and fixed, not subject to change. We need to place our attention on what we cannot see. God's Word is eternal and it is not going to change. Things are subject to change but God's Word does not change. What is unseen to us is seen by God. That's why He talks as though it is already done and *calls things which be not as though they were.*

What is unseen to us is seen by God.

Don't Get it Backwards

Sometimes, in an attempt to operate this principle, people get things mixed up and begin to operate it in reverse. They begin to call things which are as though they were not. For example, they will say, "I'm not sick. I'm not sick." Denying sickness will not heal anyone. That is not what God is teaching us.

God did not deny the darkness in Genesis 1. He did not say, "It's really not dark." Denying the darkness would never have brought light on the scene, even to this day. Denying the circumstances of life will not change them into what you desire.

God never said, "Call those things which are as though they were not." He did not say to deny what is (seen). He said to call for what is not (seen). We must call for what we do not have as though we do have it and it will be.

Imitate God

Let's examine several specific words in our text scripture found in Romans 4:17.

Notice the words "before him". In my Bible, there is a number 1 in front of those words, directing you to the cross-reference at the centre of the page. The literal translation is "like unto him". So you could read it like this: "...like him (God), who quickeneth the dead and calleth those things which be not as though they were." Paul is telling believers that we are to *be like God... who calls those things which be not as though they were.*

This is in agreement with what Paul also wrote to the Ephesians:

Ephesians 5:1
Be ye therefore followers of God, as dear children...

The Message translation says:

Ephesians 5:1, The Message
Watch what God does, and then you do it, like children who learn proper behaviour from their parents.

The Amplified translation says:

Ephesians 5:1, Amplified
Therefore be imitators of God [copy him and follow His example], as well-beloved children [imitate their father]...

...who "quickeneth the dead, and calleth those things which be not as though they were."

Notice the word 'calleth'. It means 'to summon'. According to the dictionary, the word 'summons' means 'a call by authority or the command of a superior to appear at a place named'. If you receive a summons by a court of law that means you must 'appear'. You cannot ignore it; you have no choice in the matter.

When you decree a thing and summon it in the spiritual realm, it has no choice in the matter - it must appear in the *seen* realm.

Why?

Because you have God-given authority in the earth! Jesus, the last Adam, triumphed over Satan through His death, burial and resurrection. He restored to the born-again believer all things, including authority over this earth that the first Adam lost. His victory is our victory! His anointing is our anointing! His authority is our authority!

That is exactly what God originally said to Adam:

Genesis 1:26

...and let them (Adam) have dominion (authority) over the fish of the sea, and over the fowl of the air, and over the cattle, and <u>over all the earth</u>, and over every creeping thing that creepeth upon the earth.

"Over all the earth" would include all physical matter. You are created in the very image of God. Your recreated spirit contains the same forces that reside in God: faith, love, righteousness, peace, patience, wisdom... That's why...

Thou shalt also decree a thing, and it shall be established unto thee...

28

The last words of Jesus before He left the earth were:

Matthew 28:18-19

All power (authority) is given unto me in heaven and in earth. Go ye therefore...

He transferred His authority to the believers saying, "Do what you have seen me do and say what you have seen me say." In other words, "Imitate me." Jesus' entire earthly ministry involved doing only what He saw the Father doing and speaking only what He heard the Father speaking (John 5:19, 12:49).

What was He doing?

Imitating God - *calling those things which be not as though they were* was part of that.

God has equipped us to imitate Him in order to create a life of victory and change circumstances in the earth by bringing them in line with His Word.

How?

By *calling those things which be not as though they were.*

Continuing to speak what you have will never bring what you want.

The Law of Dogs and Cats

Charles Capps is one of the most anointed Bible teachers in the world. He is also a retired farmer from my home state of Arkansas. He has a way of explaining spiritual truths in a very simple way. He has a saying: "Don't call the dog if you want the cat." For example, don't call the dog (sickness) if you want the cat (healing). If you go outside and see the dog standing there, you don't need to call the dog - he is already here. If you can't see the cat, but you want the cat to come to you, you have to call (summon) the cat. You continue to call the cat until it appears to you.

Going outside and saying, "I have the dog here," will never bring the cat. If you want the cat, you've got to call it before you will see it. Continuing to establish sickness through your words will never bring healing. Continuing to speak what you have will never bring what you want. *You must call things which be not as though they were.* You must call the cat (healing) and stop calling the dog (sickness) when it is already present. When you narrow it down to dogs and cats, it is easy to understand this spiritual principle.

God Gives the Promised Land to Israel

In Joshua 1, God appoints Joshua to lead the Israelites following the death of Moses. They are preparing to cross over the Jordan River into the Promised Land: Canaan.

Joshua 1:2-3, emphasis added

Moses my servant is dead; now therefore arise, go over this Jordan, thou, and all this people, <u>unto the land which I do give to them</u>, even to the children of Israel. Every place that the sole of your foot shall tread upon, <u>that have I given unto you</u>, as I said unto Moses.

This is a reference to what God said to Moses in Numbers 13:2. God is telling Joshua He has already given Israel the land. It belongs to them now. They have not fought one battle, they are not living there yet; and besides that, other people are currently occupying it. God is *calling those things which be not as though they (already) were.*

Numbers 13 identifies who was occupying the land at the time.

Numbers 13:29

The Amalekites dwell in the land of the south: and the Hittites, and the Jebusites, and the Amorites, dwell in the mountains: and the Canaanites dwell by the sea, and by the coast of Jordan.

In real estate terms, these people inhabited the land through adverse possession, commonly referred to as 'squatters'. Living by faith does not entitle you to just randomly go around claiming what belongs to someone else, but God had already promised this land to the nation of Israel. His Word was their title deed. (By the way, it is still Israel's title deed; I don't care what the politicians and leaders of the world think about it.)

Just because it was (and is) inhabited by someone else does not mean it belonged to the current inhabitants. Their occupancy did not give them title deed to it.

God did not tell it like it is. He did not say, "Well folks, it looks like someone else beat you to it. But if you can dispossess the current occupants, you can have it and then you can call it yours." *God called those things which be not as though they were.* Even though other people currently inhabited the land, He said He had already given it to Israel.

In Joshua 6, once again we see *God calling those things which be not as though they were.*

Joshua 6:1-2, emphasis added

Now Jericho was straitly shut up because of the children of Israel: none went out, and none came in. And the Lord said unto Joshua, <u>see, I have given into thine hand Jericho</u>, and the king thereof, and the mighty men of valour.

God then gave Joshua specific instructions on how to dispossess the inhabitants of Jericho and lay hold of the city.

Joshua 6:16, emphasis added

And it came to pass at the seventh time, when the priests blew the trumpets, Joshua said unto the people, shout: <u>For the LORD hath given you the city.</u>

Notice, God told Joshua He had already given Jericho into his hand *before* He even gave them instructions on how to take it. He did not wait until the walls had fallen and the people went in and possessed the city to tell them He was giving it to them.

God declares the end from the beginning.

While the walls were still in place and other people were living there, Joshua said to the people, *"Shout for the Lord hath (already) given you the city."*

Joshua is *calling those things which be not as though they were.* Now the only thing left for them to do was obey God's instructions and take it. In the mind of God, it already belonged to them. God was "declaring the end from the beginning". The people had to obey God and step out in faith to possess what God said already belonged to them.

The same principle still applies to your life today. *Call those things which be not as though they were...* until they are.

David Defeats Goliath

For those of us who grew up going to Sunday school, one of the first Bible stories we were ever told is the story of David and Goliath in I Samuel 17. We were told how God helped a young boy kill a huge giant who was an enemy of God. We were never told the details of *how* he did it, even though this was the key to his victory.

Sadly, there are many Christians today who grew up in Sunday school, who only know that David defeated Goliath but not *how* he defeated him. There are multiple faith principles found in the victory of David over Goliath and one of them is the principle we are focusing on in this book: *calling those things which be not as though they were.*

Let's pick up the story in I Samuel 17:

I Samuel 17:43

And the Philistine said unto David, 'Am I a dog that thou comest to me with staves?' And the Philistine cursed David by his gods.

Goliath's size alone was very intimidating and he utilized it along with his verbal threats to successfully cow down the army of Israel. David was not at all swayed by his tactics of fear. He was full of faith and did not allow what he could see and hear to change what he believed.

Then said David to the Philistine:

I Samuel 17:45

Thou comest to me with a sword, and with a spear, and with a shield: but I come to thee in the name of the LORD of hosts, the God of the armies of Israel, whom thou hast defied.

Now David is going to *call those things which be not as though they were*:

I Samuel 17:46-47, emphasis added

This day will the LORD deliver thee into mine hand; and I will smite thee, and take thine head from thee; and I will give the carcases of the host of the Philistines this day unto the fouls of the air, and to the wild beasts of the earth; that all the earth may know that there is a God in Israel. And all this assembly shall know that the LORD saveth not with sword and spear: for the battle is the LORD'S, and he will give you into our hands.

At this point, Goliath is already as good as dead. They should have started digging his grave right then. David had not even pulled a stone out of his bag and he was already telling Goliath exactly what he was going to do to him.

This day will the LORD deliver thee into mine hand... I will smite thee... I will take thine head from thee... I will give the carcases (of your entire army) this day to the fowls and wild beasts... The LORD (this day) will give you into our hands.

David actually defeated Goliath with his words. *He called those things which were not as though they were*. Then he acted on his faith by pulling out the stone that finished him off and manifested the victory. Actually, David would have killed him if he had only had a feather pillow in his hand.

Notice what David did *not* do! He did not hide behind some bushes, throw the stone, knock Goliath down, take his head off and *then* finally tell Goliath he was going to kill him. David spoke words of faith, *calling those things which be not as though they were*. His words began to operate in the unseen realm *before* the manifestation took place in the visible realm. *David spoke the desired end result first before he saw it.*

Healing

One area where Christians struggle the most with the faith principle of *calling those things which be not as though they were* is in the area of healing.

They say, "I just can't say I am healed when I can see I am not. I just can't believe something that I can't see." But they do it all of the time on the negative side of life. They will say, "I'll be the first one to get the flu when it comes around," when they are perfectly well at the time. They are calling those things which are not as though they were.

Christians have been using their faith in reverse to call for something they do not want, but because that is the way natural people in the world speak they think it is normal. They see themselves as 'sick people trying to get healed' rather than 'healed people who Satan is trying to make sick'. They 'call things that are as though they are' and keep propagating the problem they want to change.

When they use the same principle to obtain something God says already belongs to them but have no physical evidence for it, they think they are telling a lie. If you are trying to deceive someone into believing something that is not true, it would be a lie. But God's Word is true and when you are declaring what God's Word has already said about you, it cannot be a lie.

When you are in faith, the Word of God is your evidence that you have it... now.

37

When you make a statement in faith based on God's Word, it cannot be a lie, even if you can't see it yet. Healing is not even a promise - it is a fact.

I Peter 2:24

Who his own self bare our sins in his own body on the tree, that we, being dead to sins, should live unto righteousness: by whose stripes ye were healed.

Is the word 'were' past, present or future?

Peter was *calling those things which be not as though they were*. He did not say, "by whose stripes you will be healed someday" or "when you feel like it." No. He said, "by whose stripes ye *were* (already) healed."

When did this take place?

When Jesus went to the cross for us!

"But it just doesn't seem natural to say I have something I can't see or feel." If you are a born-again believer, you are not natural; you are spiritual.

In the mind of God you are already healed, just like in the mind of God, Abraham was already the father of many nations before he had any children. What is unseen to us is seen by God. You have to see yourself from God's viewpoint and speak accordingly.

> **If you are a born-again believer, you are not natural - you are spiritual.**

God's Word says you are already healed. Satan is the one trying to put sickness on you and get you to agree with him.

God says you are healed. Satan says you are not. "Why don't you feel and see if you are healed?" You are in the middle, and whoever you agree with determines the result you are going to get. You are not denying that sickness exists. You are defying sickness with the words of your mouth. You are denying sickness the right to exist in your body. You have been bought with a price - the blood of Jesus - and Satan has no right to put sickness on you when Jesus has already borne it for you on the cross.

These words should be your declaration: *"The Word of God says it; therefore I believe it. I don't have to see it to believe it."* When you are in faith, the Word of God is your evidence that you have it... now.

Jesus Applies the Same Principle

The Daughter of Abraham

In Luke 13:10-16, Jesus was teaching in one of the synagogues on the Sabbath. There was a woman present who had a spirit of infirmity and was bowed over, unable to stand up straight. She had been in this condition for eighteen years, and Jesus indicated she had been coming to the synagogue all of that time and no one had attempted to help her; at least, they had not done anything in faith for her to obtain her healing. They might have made some unbelieving, unscriptural statements and called it 'prayer'.

"Let's all remember our sister who is bowed over and can't stand up straight. If it be God's will, maybe someday she will be healed. But then God may be using this infirmity to teach her something. Let's all pray she is strong enough to bear up through it all... bless His Holy name."

That is exactly why she was stilled bowed over after eighteen years! Jesus accused the religious leaders of having more regard for their animals than for the welfare of this woman.

Luke 13:15b-16

Thou hypocrite, doth not each one of you on the Sabbath loose his ox or his ass from the stall, and lead him away to watering? And ought not this woman, being a daughter of Abraham, whom Satan hath bound, lo, these eighteen years, be loosed from this bond on the Sabbath day?

They were not interested in her being healed on any day of the week. They had had six other days of the week for eighteen years and had done nothing for her. They only wanted to split hairs over what you could and could not do on the Sabbath.

What they wanted Jesus to do was what they had been doing. If he had prayed in his most religious voice, "Faa-ther, we don't know why you put this infirmity on your child but, after all, everybody has to be sick sometime and I guess this is just her cross to bear. We know some good will come out of her suffering and it will be worth it all," all of the religious leaders would have shouted, "Amen, Hallelujah! We've got to have this young preacher at our next convention!"

But Jesus did not do what they wanted him to do. As soon as he saw her, he had compassion on her.

Did He lay hands on her and *then* say, "You are loosed" or "You are healed," after He saw she was straight?

No! He *called those things which be not as though they were.*

While she was still bowed over, Jesus said to her, "Woman, thou are loosed from thine infirmity." ("Woman, you are *already loosed* from this infirmity.")

Jesus spoke to her on the level of the Word - not on the basis of what He could see.

He said it *before* he laid his hands on her; then He saw it. He told her she was loosed when she was stilled bowed over. Not only was the ruler of the synagogue indignant because Jesus healed her on the Sabbath, he was indignant because Jesus had the audacity to say she was loosed when everyone could see she was not.

"How can you say she is already loosed when we can all see she is still bowed over?"

Was Jesus telling a lie?

Of course not! *Jesus was operating in a faith principle. He spoke to her on the level of the Word – not on the basis of what he could see.*

Jesus went on to explain, "according to the Word of God, she has a right to be loosed... she's a daughter of Abraham." (Verse 16)

He is giving us a Bible School lesson on how we must operate in faith, *calling those things which be not as though they were,* in order to change circumstances and bring them into agreement with God's Word. *He spoke the desired end result first, before he saw it.*

Jairus's Daughter

There are multiple faith principles involved in the healing of Jairus's daughter but, once again, we will focus only on the faith principle of calling those thing which be not as though they were.

Mark 5:22-23

And, behold, there cometh one of the rulers of the synagogue, Jairus by name; and when he saw him he fell at his feet, and besought him greatly, saying, My little daughter lieth at the point of death: I pray thee, come and lay thy hands on her, that she may be healed; and she shall live.

Jairus was one of the rulers of the synagogue who threw himself at the feet of Jesus on behalf of his daughter. Jairus took off his religious authority and subjected himself to the authority of Jesus. He threw himself at the feet of Jesus on behalf of his daughter who was at the point of death.

"Come and lay thy hands on her, that she may be healed; and she shall live." (Verse 23)

What a statement of faith!

I don't know exactly where Jesus was going that day but when He heard the voice of faith, He turned and followed Jairus to his home. On the way, He was interrupted by the woman with the issue of blood. She was immediately healed when she touched His garment and Jesus stopped and made her testify to what had happened to her.

By this time a messenger from Jairus's house brought news that it was too late - his daughter was dead. Let's pick up the story at verse 36.

Mark 5:36-39, emphasis added

As soon as Jesus heard the word that was spoken, he saith unto the ruler of the synagogue, 'Be not afraid, only believe.' And he suffered no man to follow him, save Peter, and James, and John the brother of James. And he cometh to the house of the ruler of the synagogue, and seeth the tumult, and them that wept and wailed greatly. And when he was come in, he saith unto them, 'Why make ye this ado, and weep? The damsel is not dead, but sleepeth.'

Verse 39 in the Greek Interlinear New Testament reads as follows:

Mark 5:39, GINT

And going in he said to them, 'Why do you make a tumult and weep? The child has not died, but is sleeping.'

Mark 5:40

And they laughed him to scorn.

I guess so! If a preacher walked into a hospital room today where a child had died and made the statement, "They have not died; they are only sleeping," they would be accused of 'denying reality' and a candidate for the insane asylum.

The doctors and family would be telling them to "get a grip on reality." But in this case, the family had *invited* Jesus into the situation and gave Him authority in the matter. Jesus ordered all of the family, friends and doctors out of the room who were in unbelief.

To Jesus, premature death was temporary and subject to change and it was not reality at all. When He said, "the child has not died, but is sleeping," was He denying reality? Was he telling a lie?

He was *calling those things which be not as though they were.* Jesus was not looking at the situation through physical eyes. He was looking through the eyes of faith. As with the woman bowed over for eighteen years, He spoke to her on the level of the Word, not on the basis of what He could see with His natural eyes.

Mark 5:41b-42

I say unto thee, arise. And straightway the damsel arose, and walked...

Let me point out once more, Jesus did not raise her up first and *then* say, "She has not died, she was only sleeping." No! He *called those things which be not as though they were* and then He gave the faith command that brought the manifestation of her healing.

He denied sickness and death the right to exist in her body. Again, *he spoke the desired end result first, before he saw it.* We should follow His example in order to obtain the same results.

The Raising of Lazarus

Let's examine another similar situation in the ministry of Jesus. Recorded in John 11 is the account of Jesus raising Lazarus from the dead. Once again, there are several faith principles involved in the raising of Lazarus, including the gift of (special) faith referred to in I Corinthians 12:9, but we will focus on the principle of *calling those things which be not as though they were*.

Lazarus and his two sisters, Mary and Martha, were personal friends of Jesus. It was this Mary who anointed the feet of Jesus with the very expensive ointment of spikenard and who was commended by Jesus in Luke 10:42 for giving her attention to the Word.

Mary and Martha sent word to Jesus that Lazarus was sick. When He received the message, He did not immediately go to him but stayed where He was for a further two days.

Let's pick up the story in verse 4.

John 11:4

When Jesus heard that, he said, 'This sickness is not unto death, but for the glory of God, that the son of God might be glorified thereby.'

Jesus did not say, "This sickness is for the glory of God." In the Bible, it is healing and restoration that always brings glory to God, not sickness and death. Sickness does not glorify anyone except Satan who is the author if it.

> **In the mind and heart of Jesus, sickness and even death were temporary and subject to change.**

Jesus was saying, "This sickness is not going to end in death." In the mind and heart of Jesus, sickness and even death were temporary and subject to change.

In verse 40, after Jesus had given instructions to roll the stone away from the tomb, Jesus said to Martha:

John 11:40

'Said I not unto thee, that, if thou wouldest believe, thou shouldest see the glory of God?'

It is obvious the glory of God referred to Lazarus being raised from the dead, restored to life and health.

John 11:11

These things said he: and after that he saith unto them, 'Our friend Lazarus sleepeth; but I go, that I may awake him out of sleep.'

Is Jesus once again denying reality?

No! *He is calling those things which be not as though they were.* Notice, Jesus would not even acknowledge death. As far as he was concerned, this situation was temporary and subject to change. Lazarus was only "sleeping".

Isn't that what He said about Jairus' daughter?

Mark 5:39

The child has not died, but is sleeping.

Because His disciples still did not understand this principle, they thought resting would be profitable for Lazarus. So why wake him up?

Jesus had to be blunt.

John 11:14

Then said Jesus unto them plainly, 'Lazarus is dead.'

Let's read this verse from the Greek Interlinear New Testament.

John 11:14, GINT

Lazarus has died.

Jesus did not actually say, "Lazarus is dead." He said, "Lazarus has died." There is a lot of difference between someone who is dead and someone who has died. Dead is permanent. Died is temporary and subject to change. Jesus died but he is not dead anymore! He died for three days and three nights but it was subject to change. It changed the course of the world for all of eternity!

Once Jesus arrived at the home of Lazarus, Martha pointed out to Him that if He had come straight away, Lazarus would not have died in the first place.

John 11:23

Jesus saith unto her, 'Thy brother shall rise again.'

Notice, Jesus did not get into a discussion with her about why He had not come or the consequences. He did not talk the problem. He only spoke the desired end result... "Thy brother shall rise again."

John 11:41

Then they took away the stone from the place where the dead man was laid. And Jesus lifted up His eyes, and said, 'Father, I thank thee that thou hast heard me.'

When did God hear him?

In verse 4 when Jesus said, "this sickness is not unto death." At that point, in the heart and mind of Jesus, Lazarus was already raised up and healed.

Once again, let me drive this point home. Jesus did not say, "Lazarus come forth" and then remark, "see there, now he is risen and this sickness was not unto death." No! He *called those things which be not as though they were.* He said, "This sickness is not unto death ... Lazarus sleepeth," *before* He gave the faith command for Lazarus to come forth.

He spoke the desired end result first, before he saw it.

You will notice a recurring theme throughout the ministry of Jesus. He never got into agreement with death. It was never a permanent situation. He did not attend funerals. He talked and acted as if death was a temporary situation and subject to change - and it was! In every case, where healings occurred and the dead were raised, He denied death the right to exist. He did not deny sickness and death; He defied it. He refused to accept it as permanent. It was subject to change.

49

In the case of Jairus' daughter, Lazarus, and the boy from Nain in Luke 7, they were not elderly believers who had lived out the full length of their lives and were satisfied, ready to go on to heaven. Jairus' daughter was only a child and they were all too young to die.

Jesus denied sickness and death the right to cut their lives short and evict them off this earth. That should also be our attitude.

The Ten Lepers

Luke 17:11-14, emphasis added

And it came to pass, as he went to Jerusalem that he passed through the midst of Samaria and Galilee. And as he entered into a certain village, there met him ten men that were lepers, which stood afar off: And they lifted up their voices, and said, 'Jesus, Master, have mercy on us.' And when he saw them, he said unto them, '<u>Go shew yourselves unto the priests.</u>' And it came to pass, that, as they went, they were cleansed.'

Now here was an opportunity for these men to miss out on their healing. What if they had said, "Jesus, can't you see we have leprosy? We can't go show ourselves to the priests as if we were healed. They will think we are denying reality. We believe in telling it like it is. We have leprosy. We can't act like we are healed when we can see that we are not. You just pray for us and when we see the leprosy is gone, then we will go show ourselves to the priests according to the scriptures."

They would most likely have never been healed because they continued to say what they had (leprosy) instead of what they wanted (healing). Healing already belonged to them and in the mind of Jesus they were already cleansed. *Jesus called things which be not as though they were.* He called them clean while they still had leprosy in their bodies.

> They did not question his method, they just got into agreement with him and acted as if they were healed.

Their obedience to put action to His instructions was their way of *calling those things which be not as though they were.* They did not question His method; they just got into agreement with Him and acted as if they were healed.

...as they went, they were cleansed.

A Withered Hand

In Mark 3, Jesus entered the synagogue in Capernaum on the Sabbath. There was a man there with a withered hand. The Bible does not indicate if he was born that way or if it was the result of an accident. Unlike the woman who was bowed over for eighteen years in Luke 13, we don't know how long his hand had been deformed. But like the woman, the religious crowd waited to see what Jesus would do on the Sabbath. As with the daughter of Abraham, they had no compassion for this man; they were only interested in another opportunity to accuse Jesus, but Jesus knew exactly what they were thinking.

Let's pick up the story in verse 3:

Mark 3:3-5

And he saith unto the man which had the withered hand, 'Stand forth.' And he saith unto them, 'Is it lawful to do good on the Sabbath days, or to do evil, to save life, or to kill?' But they held their peace. And when he had looked round about on them with anger, being grieved for the hardness of their hearts, he saith unto the man, 'Stretch forth thine hand.' And he stretched it out: and his hand was restored whole as the other.'

How did that happen?

- Because Jesus *called those things which be not as though they were!*

Did the religious folks rejoice?

- No! It made them mad.

Why?

- Because not only did Jesus heal this man on the Sabbath; He did not tell it like it is and 'call things which are as though they are'.

Jesus told him to stretch out his hand *before* there was any outward indication that it was healed. The religious folks were thinking, "Who does he think he is, telling the man to stretch out his hand? Can't he see it is withered? He tells the man to stretch out his hand as if it were normal." Jesus was looking through the eye of faith. He dealt with the man on the basis of the Word, not on the basis of what He could see with His physical eyes. *He called those things which be not as though they were.* The man received his healing because he just obeyed the Words of Jesus by faith and did as He instructed. Jesus spoke *the desired end result first, before he saw it.*

"Peace, Be Still"

Mark 4:35-39

The same day when the even was come, he saith unto them, 'Let us pass over unto the other side.' And when they had sent away the multitude, they took him even as he was in the ship. And there were also with him other little ships. And there arose a great storm of wind, and the waves beat into the ship, so that it was now full. And he was in the hinder part of the ship, asleep on a pillow: and they awake him, and say unto him, 'Master, carest thou not that we perish?' And he arose, and rebuked the wind, and said unto the sea, 'Peace, be still.' And the wind ceased, and there was a great calm.

Notice what Jesus did not do. He did not stumble out on the deck of the ship in knee-deep water and say, "You guys are right... we could all die out here... I've never seen a storm so bad on this lake before... huge waves, high winds. As soon as it calms down, come back and wake me up and then I'll say something to stop it." No!

> Jesus had to speak what they did not have in order to change what they did have.

They could have discussed how bad the storm was for hours and nothing would have changed. He had to speak what they did not have in order to change what they did have.

Jesus *called those things which be not as though they were.* He spoke *to the wind* and spoke *to the sea*, while they were still raging.

55

He spoke the desired end result first, before he saw it. He spoke words of faith in the midst of that storm. Jesus spoke what He wanted, not what He already had.

Remember the 'Law of Dogs and Cats'?

He did not wait for the wind and sea to calm down before He spoke, "Peace." That would be the same as saying, "As soon as it gets warm, I will put some wood in the fireplace." Nobody would ever say that. It would be obvious that you have to put the wood in the fireplace first, before the room warms up.

Reprogram your Mind with the Word

When it comes to applying spiritual principles to physical circumstances, Christians have difficulty understanding how they work. They want to see it or feel it first, and then say they have it. They want to "call it like it is" and then wonder why things never change.

It is because their minds have already been programmed with other sources of information other than the Word of God. Their *way* of thinking and the source of the information came from what their parents, churches, secular education, environment and culture taught them. So when they hear something from the Word of God that is spiritual, it is contrary to what and how they have already been trained to believe.

Their mind says, "Reject; we do not recognise that," just like a computer does when you enter information it has not been programmed to receive. There is nothing wrong with the information you are trying to enter and there is nothing wrong with the computer. But it will not *receive* the new information because something else has already been programmed into it that does not recognise or support what you want to input.

> Renewing your mind with the Word of God
> enables you to receive that which already
> belongs to you.

That is why born-again, Spirit-filled Christians will never walk in much faith or victory until they delete that old

57

information and *way* of thinking, and reprogram it with the Word of God. They will continue to think, talk and respond to circumstances like an unbeliever, even though their spirit is born of God. Renewing your mind with the Word of God enables you to *receive* that which already belongs to you. You begin to think, talk and respond spiritually instead of naturally.

Recreate Your World

We have examined scriptures in both the Old and New Testaments and have seen how God and Jesus both operated in the faith principle *calling those things which be not as though they were.* God said:

Malachi 3:6

'For I am the Lord, I change not...'

Jesus said:

John 5:19, 12:49

'Verily, verily, I say unto you, 'The Son can do nothing of himself, but what he seeth the Father do: for what things so ever he doeth, these also doeth the Son likewise. For I have not spoken of myself; but the Father which sent me, he gave me a commandment, what I should say, and what I should speak.'

Jesus imitated the Father; so should we.

Calling those things which be not as though they were is the spiritual principle God has operated in throughout the Bible to replace the circumstances He had with the circumstances He wanted. I can assure you He is not going to change His method now in order to accommodate our unbelief, ignorance or inconvenience. In order for our outward circumstances to change we are going to have to do things His way. That is the Word way.

That's why we are such a blessed generation to have the Word of God in every available form so we can know God's ways.

II Peter 1:3

...according as his divine power hath given unto us all things that pertain unto life and godliness, through the knowledge of him...

This is why Abraham struggled for so long and it took God a while to teach him this principle. He did not have the luxury of having a Bible like we do to learn it.

You can begin now to create a better life for yourself by using the same principle God used to create this universe.

Are there situations in your life that are contrary to the Word of God and need to be changed? Has darkness surrounded you? Be like God: *call those things which be not as though they were* and bring light into the situation.

Are there some things in your life that look like they have come to a dead end? Be like God, who 'quickeneth the dead': *call those things which be not as though they were.*

Do you have dreams and desires that have died and need to be resurrected? Do what Jesus did when He raised Lazarus from the dead: *call those things which be not as though they were* and bring them back to life.

Are you facing giants today? Do what David did: *call those things which be not as though they were* and they will fall at your feet.

Are you in the middle of a storm in your life? Do what Jesus did right in the middle of it: *call those things which be not as though they were* and bring peace on the scene.

Don't wait another day! Take authority over your circumstances and bring them into agreement with God's Word. *Call those things which be not as though they were.*

Doing the Word

Now it is time to release your faith on your circumstances.

James 1:22

But be ye doers of the word, and not hearers only, deceiving your own selves.

Just reading about the principle of *calling things that are not as though they were* might encourage you, but it is 'doing the Word' that changes things.

I have included a representative list of paraphrased scriptures to speak over your circumstances on a regular basis until the results you desire are manifested. You can also look up other scriptures that cover your specific situation.

Don't get discouraged if you do not see immediate results. The negative circumstances you may be facing today probably did not appear overnight, and it may take some time to change them.

This is not "mind-over-matter"; is it God's Word over all matter.

Light always overcomes darkness, and it doesn't matter what you are facing today. If you are diligent to do the Word and speak it in the face of your circumstances, they will have to change. It is spiritual law.

John 8:31-32

If ye continue in my Word, then are ye my disciples indeed; and ye shall know the truth, and the truth shall make you free.

Scriptural Declarations[1]

Psalm 91:10-11; Proverbs 12:28

No evil will befall me neither shall any plague come nigh my dwelling. For the Lord has given His angels charge over me and they keep me in all my ways, and in my pathway is life and there is no death.

Isaiah 54:13

I am far from oppression, and fear does not come near me.

Isaiah 54:13

Great is the peace of my children for they are taught of the Lord.

Galatians 3:13; Romans 8:11; Genesis 1:31; Matthew 16:19

Christ has redeemed me from the curse of the law. Therefore, I forbid any sickness or disease to come upon this body. Every disease germ and every virus that touches this body dies instantly in the name of Jesus. Every organ and every tissue of this body functions in the perfection to which God created it to function, and I forbid any malfunction in this body, in the name of Jesus.

---

[1] Scripture declarations from *God's Creative Power*®, pages 17-21, 25, by Charles Capps.

Psalms 23:1; 2 Corinthians 8:9; John 10:10

The Lord is my shepherd and I do not want. Jesus was made poor, that I through His poverty might have abundance. For he came that I might have life and have it more abundantly.

Philippians 4:19

There is no lack for my God supplies all of my need according to His riches in glory by Christ Jesus.

Colossians 3:15

I let the peace of God rule in my heart and I refuse to worry about anything.

2 Corinthians 6:16; John 10:10; II Peter 1:3-4; Romans 8:31

God is on my side. God is in me now, who can be against me? He has given unto me all things that pertain unto life and godliness. Therefore I am a partaker of His divine nature.

Matthew 6:12; Romans 5:5

I am free from unforgiveness and strife. I forgive others as Christ has forgiven me, for the love of God is shed abroad in my heart by the Holy Ghost.

Psalms 118:17

Jesus bore my sickness and carried my pain. Therefore I give no place to sickness or pain. For God sent His Word and healed me.

Psalms 118:17

I will not die but live and declare the works of God.

Luke 6:38

As I give, it is given unto me, good measure, pressed down, shaken together, and running over.

Prayer of Salvation

If you do not know JESUS as your Saviour and Lord, simply pray the following prayer in faith from your heart and Jesus will be your Lord:

> *Heavenly Father, your Word says that "whoever calls on the name of the Lord shall be saved and if I confess with my mouth the Lord Jesus and believe in my heart that God has raised Him from the dead, I shall be saved." (Acts 2:21, Romans 10:9)*
>
> *I believe your Word and I confess Jesus as Lord.*
>
> *I believe in my heart that Jesus died on the cross for my sins and that You raised Him from the dead.*
>
> *Jesus, I ask you to come into my heart right now and fill me with your Holy Spirit.*
>
> *I receive You as my Lord and Saviour.*
>
> *Take my life and do something with it.*
>
> *Amen.*

If you have just prayed this prayer from your heart, your spirit is now born anew by the Spirit of God. You can now receive all that Jesus died on the cross to give you. You are now a partaker of the divine nature through the exceeding great and precious promises in the Word of God (II Peter 1:4). God designed a unique and perfect plan for your life. As you put the Word of God into first place and are led by the Spirit of God, you will find yourself living in that wonderful plan.

Welcome to the Family of God!

Please contact us at the address below and let us know of your decision.

Barb Witt Ministries
P.O. Box 495
Godalming,
Surrey
GU7 2WB

barbwitt1@gmail.com
www.barbwitt.org

From the Publisher

Titles in the **Timeless Teaching** series:

1.	What do These Stones Mean?	*Joyce Sibthorpe*
2.	Motherhood	*Diana Jeffery*
3.	A Walk with Wisdom	*Luke Jeffery*
4.	Four Mountains to Climb Before you Die	*Mark Jeffery*
5.	Can You Hear God?	*Joyce Sibthorpe*
6.	The Christian Guide to Jobs and Careers	*Charles Humphries*
7.	Alive for a Purpose	*Kofi Owusu*
8.	Equipped to Heal	*Dr. Ian Andrews*
9.	Diagnosing Ills and Ailments of Relationships	*Adedeji Majekodunmi*
10.	Pursuing Holiness	*Sam Masamba*
11.	Single without Sinking	*Shade Vaughan*
12.	Redeeming a Nation	*Philip Quenby*
13.	Calling Things that Are Not as though They Were	*Barb Witt*

Books available from the publisher:
www.onwardsandupwards.org